Contents

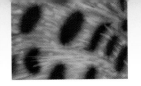

Meet the Cheetah

Cheetahs are sleek, graceful big cats. Streamlined hunters, with long legs and powerful muscles, they can run faster than any other animal in the world. They live alone or in small groups, in the dry, flat grasslands of Africa and Asia.

Cheetahs belong to the same family as lions, tigers and leopards, but they look slightly different. Their bodies are lighter and thinner, and they have smaller heads. Like leopards, cheetahs have spots. But unlike a leopard, a cheetah has black 'tear marks' on its face.

CHEETAH FACTS

Cheetahs grow up to 1.3 metres long. This does not include the tail, which can be up to 80 centimetres long. Males are slightly bigger than females.

●

A cheetah weighs 35–60 kilograms.

●

There is only one species (type) of cheetah. Its Latin name is *Acinonyx jubatus*. The name 'cheetah' comes from an old Hindu word, *chita*, meaning 'spotty'.

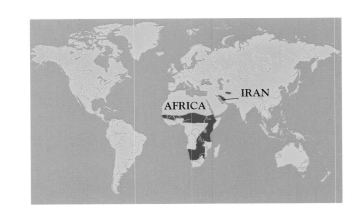

▶ The red shading on this map shows where cheetahs live. Most cheetahs are found in Africa, but a few also live in Iran.

NATURAL WORLD

CHEETAH

HABITATS • LI... • THREATS

Anna Claybourne

HODDER
Wayland

an imprint of Hodder
Children's Books

WWF

Produced in Association with WWF-UK

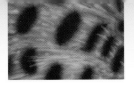

NATURAL WORLD

Black Rhino • Cheetah • Chimpanzee • Crocodile • Dolphin
Giant Panda • Giraffe • Golden Eagle • Gorilla • Great White Shark
Hippopotamus • Kangaroo • Koala • Leopard • Moose
Orangutan • Penguin • Polar Bear • Seal • Tiger • Wolf • Zebra

Produced for Hodder Wayland by
Monkey Puzzle Media Ltd
Gissing's Farm, Fressingfield
Suffolk IP21 5SH, UK

Produced in association with WWF-UK.
WWF-UK registered charity number
1081247. A company limited by guarantee
number 4016725. Panda device © 1986 WWF.
® WWF registered trademark owner.

Cover: Face to face with a cheetah.
Title page: A cheetah stands alert, watching for prey.
Contents page: A cheetah sits in the sun in the Masai Mara
National Park in Kenya, Africa.
Index page: Three cheetah cubs play together, hiding from their
mother behind a log.

Published in Great Britain in 2003 by Hodder Wayland,
an imprint of Hodder Children's Books
Text copyright © 2003 Hodder Wayland
Volume copyright © 2003 Hodder Wayland
This paperback edition published in 2004

Hodder Children's Books
A division of Hodder Headline Limited
338 Euston Road, London NW1 3BH

Editor: Angela Wilkes
Series editor: Victoria Brooker
Designer: Sarah Crouch

British Library Cataloguing in Publication Data
Claybourne, Anna
  Cheetah. - (Natural world)
  1.Cheetah - Juvenile literature
  I.Title
  599.7'59

ISBN 0 7502 4244 2

Printed in China

Picture acknowledgements
Alamy front cover (Gary Cook); Karl Ammann 12, 19,
39, 40; *Bridgeman Art Library* 7 (Manchester City
Galleries); *FLPA* 1 (Winifried Wisniewski), 22
(Winifried Wisniewski), 30 (Peter Davey), 32 (Fritz
Polking), 34 (Minden Pictures), 37 (Tom and Pam
Gardner), 41 (Fritz Polking), 43 (G Marcoaldi/Panda
Photo), 45 middle (Tom and Pam Gardner), 45 bottom
(Fritz Polking); *Nature Picture Library* 3 (Simon King),
8 (Bruce Davidson), 15 (Anup Shah), 16 (Anup Shah),
17 (Anup Shah), 20 (Anup Shah), 21 (Anup Shah), 23
(Richard du Toit), 24 (Anup Shah), 27 (Anup Shah),
29 (Anup Shah), 36 (Peter Blackwell), 44 bottom
(Anup Shah), 48 (Anup Shah); *NHPA* 6 (Martin
Harvey), 9 (Christophe Ratier), 13 (Martin Harvey),
18 (Nigel J Dennis), 26 (Martin Harvey), 28
(Christophe Ratier), 33 (Kevin Schafer), 35 (Anthony
Bannister), 38 (Martin Harvey), 42 (Daryl Balfour), 45
top (Nigel J Dennis); *Oxford Scientific Films* 10 (Rob
Nunnington), 11 (Norbert Rosing), 25 (Norbert
Rosing), 44 top (Rob Nunnington), 44 middle
(Norbert Rosing); *Still Pictures* 14 (M and C Denis-
Huot). Artwork by Michael Posen.

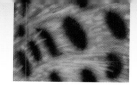

▼ An adult female cheetah

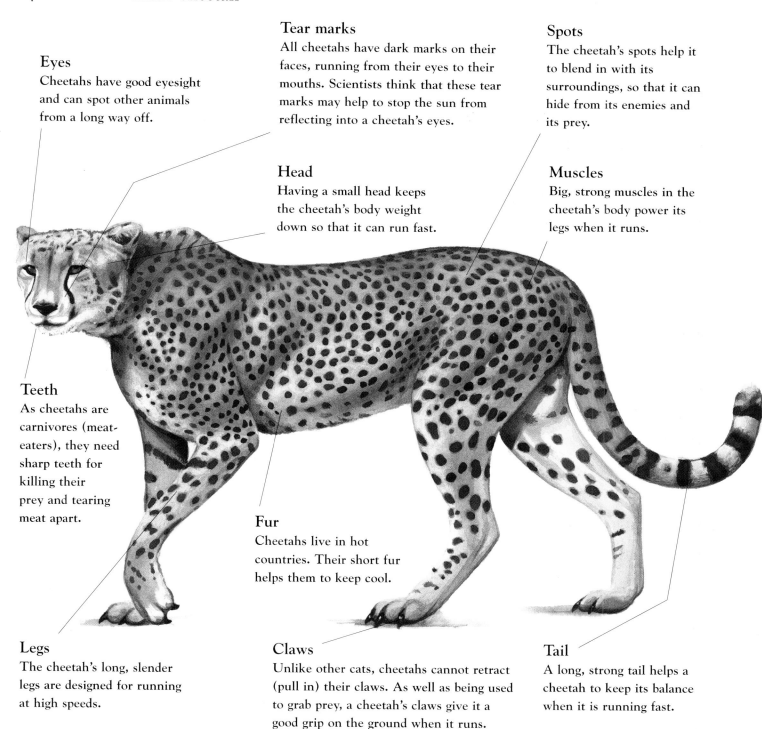

Eyes
Cheetahs have good eyesight and can spot other animals from a long way off.

Tear marks
All cheetahs have dark marks on their faces, running from their eyes to their mouths. Scientists think that these tear marks may help to stop the sun from reflecting into a cheetah's eyes.

Spots
The cheetah's spots help it to blend in with its surroundings, so that it can hide from its enemies and its prey.

Head
Having a small head keeps the cheetah's body weight down so that it can run fast.

Muscles
Big, strong muscles in the cheetah's body power its legs when it runs.

Teeth
As cheetahs are carnivores (meat-eaters), they need sharp teeth for killing their prey and tearing meat apart.

Fur
Cheetahs live in hot countries. Their short fur helps them to keep cool.

Legs
The cheetah's long, slender legs are designed for running at high speeds.

Claws
Unlike other cats, cheetahs cannot retract (pull in) their claws. As well as being used to grab prey, a cheetah's claws give it a good grip on the ground when it runs.

Tail
A long, strong tail helps a cheetah to keep its balance when it is running fast.

A long history

Cheetahs have existed for four million years. Of all the big cats living on Earth today, cheetahs were the first to evolve. Fossils show that they used to live in Europe and North America as well as Africa and Asia.

▼ The king cheetah is one of the seven subspecies of cheetah. Some of its spots are joined together, giving it extra-large, blob-shaped spots and short stripes.

▲ This picture of a cheetah and two Indians was painted in 1765 by the English artist George Stubbs. The men are about to send the cheetah to chase a stag.

CHEETAH GODDESS

The ancient Egyptian goddess Mafdet was often shown in the form of a cheetah.

There were once several different species of cheetah, but most of them died out when the last Ice Age ended, about 10,000 years ago. There is now just one species left, with seven subspecies (slightly different types) within it. Although there are some differences between them, all the cheetahs living today are thought to have descended from the same parents and are closely related to each other.

In the past, cheetahs were kept as pets and hunting companions in royal households. Akbar the Great, who was Emperor of India from 1556 to 1605, kept over 9,000 cheetahs during his reign.

Where cheetahs live

Cheetahs live in grasslands – wide, open spaces covered in grass and dotted with a few trees and rocks. There are grasslands all over the world, but cheetahs are only found in those in hot, dry places, especially Africa. The grasslands in Africa are known as savannahs.

Cheetahs have adapted well to life in these surroundings. Being able to run fast means that they can chase animals like gazelles across the open savannah. They use rocky outcrops and trees as lookout points to scan the savannah for prey. Their yellow fur and spots provide good camouflage as they move stealthily through the tawny dry grass.

▼ This picture shows a typical savannah in Kenya in eastern Africa. Although there are mountains in the distance, the savannah itself is very flat, with dry brown grass and a few bushes and trees.

Many cheetahs now live on farmland. This is because large areas of former grassland are being turned into farms. The cheetahs have nowhere else to go, so they live in the fields among farm animals. This can cause problems.

▲ This cheetah has climbed up on to a rock to get a good view of the surrounding savannah. From here, it's easier to spot prey animals.

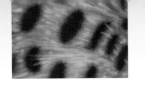

A Cheetah is Born

▲ These two tiny cheetah cubs are only five days old. Their eyes are still closed and their fur is much darker than an adult cheetah's. However, it's easy to tell they are cheetahs, as they already have their tear marks.

When a pregnant cheetah is ready to have her babies, she finds a quiet place tucked out of sight. It might be a gap between some rocks, or a space under a bush. There she gives birth to a litter of between two and five cubs.

Newborn cheetah cubs do not look like their parents. Their fur is darker, and they have a woolly grey mane along their backs, called a mantle. At first, they are very weak and helpless. They have no teeth, and their eyes are tightly shut. Their mother licks them clean and watches over them. Like other mammals, baby cheetahs feed on milk from their mother at first.

Male and female cheetahs only meet up to mate. The father leaves long before the cubs are born, so the mother looks after her cubs by herself. They will stay with her for up to two years.

▼ A litter of five three-week-old cubs feeding on their mother's milk.

CHEETAH CUB FACTS

A mother cheetah is pregnant for about three months before giving birth.

●

Newborn cheetah cubs are about 30 centimetres long and weigh 200–300 grams.

●

There can be up to eight cubs in a litter.

●

Cheetah cubs open their eyes when they are one week old, and can walk a week later.

11

DANGER EVERYWHERE

Several dangers threaten cheetah cubs as they are growing up. They may be attacked by lions, hyenas or jackals. They are also in danger from snakes, which kill their prey with poisonous bites or squeeze them to death. Cheetahs are more likely to catch diseases than other cats. Lastly, finding food is hard, even for fierce hunters, and some cheetah cubs starve to death.

Dangerous days

The first few weeks of a cheetah's life are very risky. The mother cheetah has to leave her cubs to go hunting. At first, she just looks for food for herself, but later she needs meat to bring back to the cubs. While she is away, her cubs are in danger of being attacked and eaten by lions, hyenas and other hungry predators. And if the mother cheetah does not find enough food, the cubs may die of starvation.

▲ This cub has been left in a crack between two rocks, so that it is well hidden while its mother goes hunting.

In an attempt to keep her cubs safe, the mother cheetah moves them to a new hiding place almost every day. This confuses predators and makes it hard for them to track the cubs down by their scent. The cubs' fluffy mantles may also help to keep them safe by giving them extra camouflage among the grass.

◀ These cubs are staying close to their mother for safety. You can clearly see their woolly manes or 'mantles'.

However, because of all the dangers facing them, fewer than half of all cheetah cubs make it to adulthood. In some areas, nine out of ten cubs die before they are five months old.

First food

When cheetah cubs are just a few weeks old, their mother starts to feed them meat as well as milk. At first she regurgitates food for them. This means that she brings up chewed meat from her stomach and lets them eat it. Many animals do this for their babies.

STAGES IN A CUB'S LIFE

- Newborn: the cub starts feeding on milk.
  - 1 week old: its eyes open.
  - 2 weeks old: it learns to walk.
- 3-4 weeks old: it starts eating regurgitated meat.
  - 6 weeks old: it starts following its mother on hunts.
  - 3 months old: it stops feeding on milk.
  - 4 months old: it starts losing its mantle.

◀ At two months old, this cheetah cub is brave enough to start exploring its surroundings and has climbed a small tree.

When they are six to eight weeks old, the cubs are big enough to come out to play. They start to follow their mother when she goes hunting, and learn to eat fresh meat straight from the carcass (the body of a dead animal). Cheetah cubs are very playful. They love to stalk flowers and insects, chase each other and jump on their mother's back.

By the time they are three to four months old, the cubs are weaned, which means they stop feeding on their mother's milk. Their woolly grey manes gradually get smaller, and they start to look like small adults.

▲ Two cubs play at hiding from each other behind their mother. These cubs are from the litter shown on page 48.

Learning to Survive

When cheetah cubs are about six months old, they have to start learning how to look after themselves, so their mother trains them to hunt. She catches a small animal, such as a hare or a young gazelle, but does not kill it. Instead she gives it to the cubs, so that they can practise chasing it and pouncing on it. They also learn to kill prey by biting its throat.

CHEETAH CHATTER

Cheetahs never roar like other big cats. They can only make quieter noises, which sound like little squeaks, chirrups and grunts.

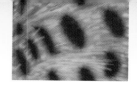

▲ A mother cheetah licks one of her cubs clean after a meal.

◀ A group of cubs chase and pounce on a young gazelle their mother has caught for them, while she watches from the sidelines.

This might sound cruel, but chasing and killing other animals is the only way cheetahs can survive. Like other members of the cat family, they are designed to live on meat and very little else. If they are to survive on their own, the cubs must become fierce hunters.

After feeding, the mother and cubs often lie down together to relax. They lick and groom each other, and make chirping and purring noises.

Getting bigger

By the age of eight or nine months, the cheetah cubs have grown nearly as big as their mother, and they are no longer in danger from predators. Their teeth and claws are fully grown and they can run fast enough to escape from any animal that chases them.

▲ This young cheetah still has fluffy fur and a baby face, but has lost most of its mantle. It has learned to stand still and alert like an adult to watch for prey.

However, they will still stay with their mother for a few more months. Most cheetah cubs live with their mother for at least a year, and some stay for up to two years. They continue to perfect their hunting skills until they can hunt like an adult cheetah. That means learning how to spot prey from a long way off, creep up on herds of antelopes or zebras, and keep up a high-speed chase.

The young cheetahs also spend a lot of time play-fighting, climbing trees and rolling in the grass.

▼ Even though they are nearly a year old, these young cheetahs still love play-fighting with each other.

Leaving home

By 15 months old, the cheetahs have reached their full adult size. Their fluffy mantles have completely disappeared. Their fur is sandy yellow with black spots, their stomachs and throats are white, and their tails are striped black and yellow with a white tip. They can run at full cheetah speed and catch their own prey. When they are one to two years old, young cheetahs are finally ready to leave home.

▲ A group of young cheetahs on the prowl together.

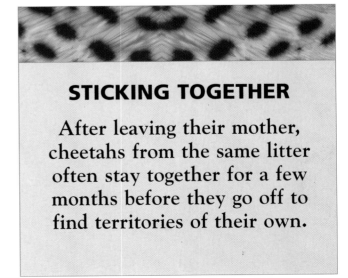

STICKING TOGETHER

After leaving their mother, cheetahs from the same litter often stay together for a few months before they go off to find territories of their own.

Despite all their training, though, they will face a struggle to survive. Each cheetah needs its own space, called a territory, to live in. Territories have to be large, because they must contain enough prey animals for a cheetah to live on. But because wild grassland is becoming scarce, it's hard for young cheetahs to find good territories.

▼ For cheetahs to survive in the wild, they need a large area of open grassland like this, with lots of animals living in it. In this picture you can see giraffes and wildebeest.

Males and females

Young male and female cheetahs behave differently. Male cheetahs often stay together and live in a small group of two or three animals. They find themselves a territory a long way away from the place they grew up – sometimes up to 300 kilometres away. They hunt together and gang up to defend their territory from other animals and other cheetahs.

Some males do live on their own. Instead of guarding a small territory, they tend to be nomadic, which means that they wander long distances in search of food.

▲ After growing up playing with their siblings, many cheetahs have to find a place to live by themselves, especially females.

▶ This cheetah is marking its territory with urine (wee). The smell of the urine will warn other cheetahs that this territory is already taken.

Once young females leave their family group, they usually live and hunt on their own until they mate and have cubs. However, they do not move such a long way away, and are not as keen to guard their territory as males are. Mother and sister cheetahs often have large territories that overlap with each other.

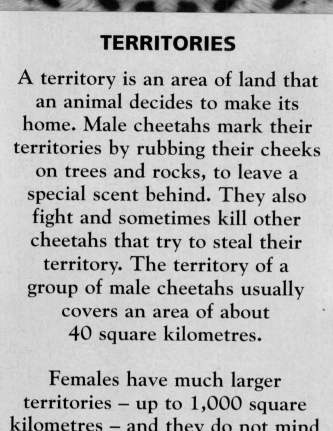

TERRITORIES

A territory is an area of land that an animal decides to make its home. Male cheetahs mark their territories by rubbing their cheeks on trees and rocks, to leave a special scent behind. They also fight and sometimes kill other cheetahs that try to steal their territory. The territory of a group of male cheetahs usually covers an area of about 40 square kilometres.

Females have much larger territories – up to 1,000 square kilometres – and they do not mind sharing them. Females and males meet up to mate where male and female territories overlap slightly.

23

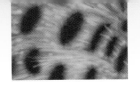

Finding Food

A cheetah's body is a highly specialized killing machine. It has many adaptations for chasing and catching other animals. Cheetahs have two sets of leg muscles. They use one for normal walking, and the other for running at high speed. A cheetah's flexible back works like a spring, powering the cat's massive leaps, while its long tail is used for balance. As well as their normal claws, which grip the ground while running, cheetahs have a special sharp claw called a dewclaw on each foot. This is used to hook on to prey and pull it down.

▼ When a cheetah opens its mouth to yawn, you can see its teeth clearly. The two long pointed teeth are the canine teeth, used for tearing and cutting meat. They are smaller than those of most other big cats.

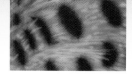

CHEETAH TEETH

Unlike some cats, cheetahs don't have especially big teeth. While tigers and lions gobble their food and crunch on bones and skin, cheetahs nibble delicately at their prey and only eat the meat. They also eat smaller prey than most big cats.

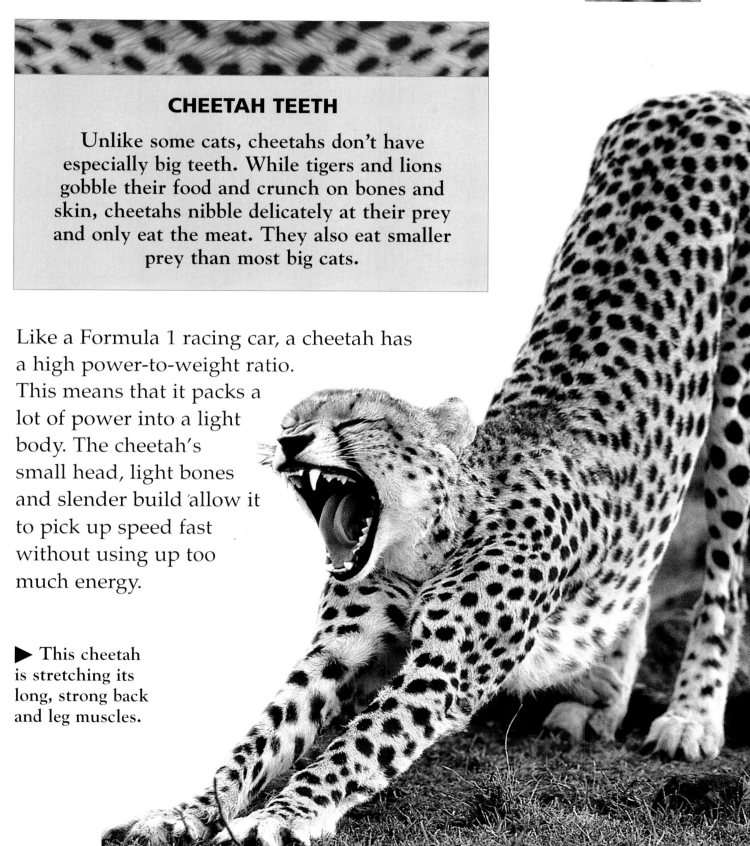

Like a Formula 1 racing car, a cheetah has a high power-to-weight ratio. This means that it packs a lot of power into a light body. The cheetah's small head, light bones and slender build allow it to pick up speed fast without using up too much energy.

▶ This cheetah is stretching its long, strong back and leg muscles.

Detecting and stalking

Unlike most cats, cheetahs often hunt during the day. This is because they chase their prey over quite long distances, which would be hard to do in the dark. Other cats, such as tigers, hunt at night and pounce on their victims from close range.

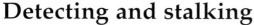 ► A cheetah keeps its body low to the ground as it stalks closer to its prey.

◄ This cheetah is using a termite mound as a lookout point. Termites are similar to ants. Their large nests, made out of soil, can be several metres high, making them perfect places from which to scan the savannah.

Before it can begin a chase, a cheetah needs to locate its prey in the vast savannah. The animals the cheetah hunts, such as antelopes, are often well camouflaged and hard to spot. But a cheetah has very good eyesight. It scans the horizon from a vantage point on a rock or a tree branch, looking for herds of animals moving across the grass.

When it sees something of interest, such as a herd of gazelles, a cheetah casually walks towards them. As it gets nearer, it crouches down and stalks closer and closer, until it's only about 50 metres away from the herd and ready to attack.

EARS AND NOSES

Like other cats, cheetahs have a good sense of smell and sensitive ears. These senses help them find prey, but because cheetahs hunt in daylight, hearing is not as important for finding food as eyesight. Smell and hearing are more useful for finding a mate.

In for the kill

When the cheetah is close enough to a herd of gazelles or other prey, it selects one animal to chase. This is often the one that starts moving first. Scientists are not sure why. Cheetahs rarely pick weak or injured animals, even though they would have a better chance of catching them.

The cheetah suddenly charges towards its target and the gazelle starts running for its life. The cheetah can keep up the chase, at a speed of around 70 kilometres per hour, for several kilometres. Its eyes are spaced wide apart and this helps it to keep track of the gazelle as it bounds this way and that, trying to escape.

▲ This cheetah is closing in on its prey, a young gazelle. Gazelles try to escape by darting from side to side, but the cheetah can change direction just as fast.

▶ Finally, the cheetah catches up with its unlucky prey and pulls it to the ground.

TOP SPEEDS

The cheetah is the fastest animal on land. Other fast runners include the pronghorn antelope (98 kilometres per hour), the wildebeest and springbok (both 80 kilometres per hour) and Thomson's gazelle (76 kilometres per hour). The zebra is a little slower, but can still run as fast as a greyhound, with a top speed of 65 kilometres per hour.

The chase ends with a final short burst of speed of up to 113 kilometres per hour. The cheetah is now covering seven metres with each leap. Finally, it strikes. If it is close enough, it knocks or drags the gazelle down with its claws, and clamps its jaws around its neck to stop it from breathing.

However, cheetahs only catch their prey about half of the time. Although gazelles and other prey animals cannot run as fast as a cheetah, they have a good chance of escaping if they can get a head start and keep running until the cheetah is exhausted.

Mealtimes

After making a kill, a cheetah has to act fast. Other animals, such as hyenas and lions, will move in and steal the food if they can. So the cheetah pulls the carcass into some bushes, or even up a tree, and quickly eats as much of it as possible. If the cheetah is a mother with cubs, she may drag her kill away to share with them instead.

FAVOURITE FOODS

Cheetahs eat many different kinds of animal. Their favourites include Thomson's gazelles, impalas, springboks and other antelopes, young warthogs and wildebeest, hares and birds. Some cheetahs have even been known to lure birds by imitating their calls.

◀ A cheetah drags its victim, a wildebeest calf, into the bushes before eating it.

▼ This food chain shows some of the foods a cheetah eats and some of the predators that threaten cheetahs.

A cheetah can eat up to 14 kilograms of meat per meal. When it has finished eating, other animals, including jackals, vultures and ants, will pick at the carcass and eat whatever is left behind. Animals that eat other animals' leftovers in this way are called scavengers.

CHEETAH FOOD CHAIN

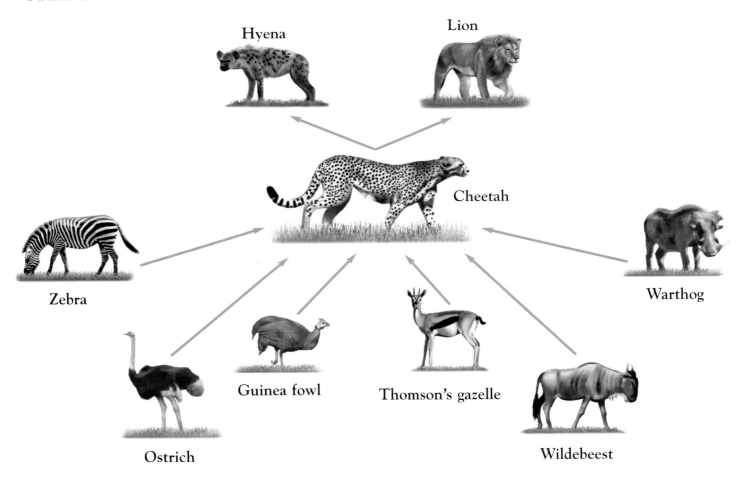

Hyena

Lion

Cheetah

Zebra

Guinea fowl

Ostrich

Thomson's gazelle

Wildebeest

Warthog

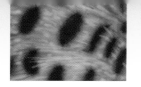

Adult Life

A cheetah's life consists mainly of hunting, eating and snoozing. Most other cats are nocturnal, which means that they are active mainly at night. But cheetahs come out in the early morning and late afternoon, as well as on moonlit nights. They often go to sleep in the middle of the day, sometimes up a tree.

▼ A mother cheetah and one of her cubs rest during the hottest time of the day.

Cheetahs don't hunt every single day, unless they are mothers with a family to feed. Most cheetahs only make a kill every three to five days. They eat as much as they can straight away, and then don't eat again until their next kill.

Every four or five days, a cheetah also has to visit watering holes or rivers to have a drink. In some parts of Africa, though, cheetahs get some of the liquid they need from eating melons. This means that they can go without water for up to ten days.

▲ A cheetah has a drink of water after eating a meal. Like other cats, cheetahs lap up water using their rough tongues.

Season to season

Some cheetahs, particularly those that live alone, are nomadic. They move around a lot, depending on the season, to wherever they can find food.

▲ Where there is not much cover and not much prey, it's hard for a cheetah to have a permanent territory.

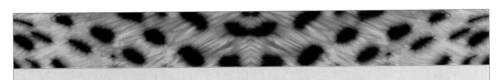

MYSTERIOUS MOBBING

Sometimes, animals such as giraffes, gazelles and birds get into a group and follow a cheetah. This is called mobbing. Scientists are not sure why it happens, but they think it helps prey animals to keep safe by sticking together and keeping an eye on the cheetah. It may also help other prey animals to see the cheetah coming.

This happens most of all in the Serengeti National Park in Tanzania, East Africa. It has a rainy season from November to May, and a dry season from June to October. In the rainy season, grazing animals such as gazelles and wildebeest feed in the south of the park. In the dry season, the southern areas dry out. There is no longer much to eat or drink there, so the animals migrate north again. As cheetahs feed on these species, they follow them as they move, travelling hundreds of kilometres every year.

Some cheetahs also mate according to the seasons. More cubs are born in the rainy season, because it's easier to find food then.

▼ These wildebeest are migrating across the savannah in search of food and water. Wherever they go, they will be followed by cheetahs which need to be close to their prey.

35

Finding a mate

As male and female cheetahs normally live apart, they have to find each other in order to mate and have babies. When a female is ready to mate, she gives off a special scent. Male cheetahs can smell it and come to find the female. Females fight off males they are not interested in, and males sometimes fight each other over a female. Finally, the female chooses the male she wants.

▶ A male and female cheetah rest together and lick each other before mating.

▼ These two cheetahs are fighting, possibly over a mate. Cheetah fights can be so vicious that they end up with one of the cheetahs dying.

BABY COUNT

In her lifetime a female cheetah could have four to five litters, and give birth to more than 20 cubs. Most females have fewer cubs, and only half of those that are born will survive to adulthood.

The male and the female spend up to a week together, and mate several times to make sure the female gets pregnant. Then the male goes away again, leaving the female cheetah to give birth and raise her cubs alone. Males do not usually see their cubs or help to look after them.

Each litter of cubs takes up to two years to raise to adulthood. As soon as they leave home the female is ready to mate again.

A LIFE OF LEISURE

In captivity, cheetahs live for longer because they don't have to catch their own food or fight other animals for it. So cheetahs in zoos often live for 12 years or more.

◀ This cheetah is wearing a special collar that sends out radio signals. The cheetah usually has to be caught and drugged while the collar is put on.

▲ Birds of prey feed on the carcass (dead body) of a cheetah. It won't be long before it is joined by more vultures and other scavengers.

Old age and death

Scientists have radio-tracked cheetahs to find out how long they live. They give a cheetah a collar or tag that sends out radio signals. By collecting the signals, they can find out where the cheetah is and keep track of it. They have found that in the wild, the average cheetah only lives to the age of seven.

Unlike humans, cheetahs cannot survive at all if they grow old and frail, or get an injury. They depend on their high speed and alert senses to find food. As soon as a cheetah starts to age, its muscles and eyesight get weaker. It can no longer catch and kill a fast animal like a gazelle, or defend its kill from hungry hyenas or jackals. So it will probably starve to death. Sometimes, hyenas even attack and kill an old, weak cheetah.

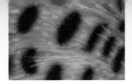

Threats

Cheetahs are endangered, which means they are in danger of dying out and becoming extinct. There are several reasons for this.

Firstly, the wild grasslands where cheetahs live are being turned into farms, roads and towns. When this happens, cheetahs cannot always find enough of their natural food. If they eat farm animals instead, farmers sometimes shoot them. To make matters worse, some people hunt cheetahs for their skins, even though it's against the law.

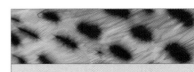

DO CHEETAHS EAT HUMANS?

Although cheetahs are big, fierce hunters, they hardly ever hurt humans. A cheetah would only bite you if you threatened it or went too close to its cubs.

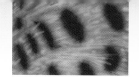

▲ A cheetah lies fatally wounded after a fight with a leopard.

Cheetahs also suffer from a lot of diseases, which kill hundreds of them every year. Lastly, they are weaker than other big cats, such as lions, and they are not very good at fighting them. Even in a national park, where animals are protected from hunters, cheetahs are at risk from other animals stealing their prey and killing their cubs.

◄ A cheetah approaches a lion that has invaded its territory. Unfortunately for the cheetah, if the two cats fight, the lion will probably win.

Because of all these problems, experts think there are now fewer than 10,000 wild cheetahs left. The species could be completely extinct by the year 2020 unless continued conservation efforts are made to protect cheetahs and their habitats.

ADOPT A CHEETAH

You can help with cheetah conservation by adopting a cheetah. You send some money to a conservation charity, and it is used to look after a cheetah in a breeding station, zoo or reserve.
Turn to page 47 for more information on cheetah charities that can help you adopt a cheetah.

Cheetah conservation

Many countries and organisations are now trying to 'conserve' or save cheetahs, so that they don't die out. Africa has lots of large national parks and wildlife reserves where cheetahs are protected from poachers. Tourists can pay to go and see the cheetahs and other wildlife, instead of hunting them.

▲ A cheetah relaxes in Chobe National Park in Botswana, southern Africa.

Zoos can often help with conservation by breeding endangered animals. But cheetahs are very hard to breed in captivity. In fact, they do so badly that even though Akbar of India kept 9,000 cheetahs, he only ever managed to breed one litter of cubs. Things are not much better in zoos today.

Instead, some cheetahs are bred on breeding stations in Africa. They are like big farms with lots of open space for cheetahs to live as they do in the wild, without the threat of predators. There are also schemes to train farm dogs to protect livestock, so that farmers don't need to kill cheetahs.

▼ Some charities are trying to save cheetahs by training dogs to guard farm animals. The dogs keep predators such as cheetahs away, but do not kill them.

Cheetah Life Cycle

 **1** Newborn cheetahs have dark fur and a fluffy 'mantle'. Their eyes are closed and they can't walk.

 **2** The cubs feed on their mother's milk for the first few weeks. Their eyes open after a week and they learn to walk when they are two weeks old.

 **3** From six weeks old, young cheetahs follow their mother and learn to chase and kill prey.

 Cubs leave their mother when they are one to two years old and find their own territory or living space.

 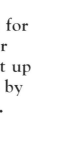 From the age of two for females and three for males, cheetahs meet up to mate. The female raises the cubs by herself, with no help from the male.

 In the wild, cheetahs live to about seven years old. They may be killed by predators or starve when they can no longer catch food.

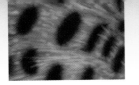

SCIENCE
- Grassland ecosystems and food webs
- Animal classification: mammals and big cats
- Adaptation to habitat: cheetah's body shape
- How predators use senses
- How animals keep cool

ENGLISH AND LITERACY
- Scientific and common names for animals
- Poetry: write poems on the thrill of the chase

GEOGRAPHY
- Mapwork: where do cheetahs live?
- Find out about people who live in grasslands
- Tourism: safaris
- Migration to find food

Cheetah Topic Web

MATHS
- Compare top speeds of different animals
- Statistics: counting how many animals are left

ICT
- Web searching: cheetah charities and facts

ART
- Camouflage patterns
- Showing speed in art

HISTORY
- Royal household animals of the past
- Akbar the Great of India

Extension Activities

English
- Debate which is more important: cheetahs' lives or farmers' livelihoods.
- Talk about words to describe big cats; the way they look, sound and move.
- Write a story about living on a farm where cheetahs are stealing the sheep.
- Write a letter to a Martian explaining what a cheetah is.

Geography
- Draw a map of Africa and the Middle East, showing where cheetahs live.
- Find out which countries have the most cheetahs living in them.

Maths
- Work out how long it would take a cheetah running at full speed to travel from your home to your school.

Science
- Make a 'radio-tracking' map of your area showing where you travel in a day.
- Find out about Ice Ages and when the last one was.

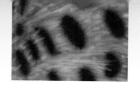

Glossary

Adapting Changing over time to suit the surroundings and the food available.
Camouflage Colours, patterns and shapes that help an animal to blend in with its surroundings.
Conservation Trying to keep our planet healthy by saving endangered species, reducing pollution, and so on.
Endangered At risk of dying out.
Evolve To change and develop over a period of time.
Extinct An extinct animal has died out completely and no longer exists.
Fossil The remains of a prehistoric animal or plant that have been hardened into rock.
Habitat The natural home of a living thing.

Litter A group of cubs all born to the same mother at the same time.
Mantle The mane of fluffy hair on a young cheetah's head and back.
Migrate To travel long distances according to the season.
Nocturnal Active mainly at night.
Predator An animal that hunts and kills other animals.
Prey An animal that is hunted and killed by other animals.
Solitary Preferring to live alone.
Species The scientific name for a type of living thing.
Territory An area that an animal lives in and defends as its own.

Further Information

Organizations to Contact

WWF-UK
Panda House, Weyside Park
Godalming, Surrey GU7 1XR
Tel: 01483 426444
Website: www.wwf-uk.org

Cheetah Conservation Fund
PO Box 1380
Ojai, CA, USA 93024
Tel: +1 (805) 640-0390
Website: www.cheetah.org

Books to Read

Built for Speed: The Extraordinary, Enigmatic Cheetah by Sharon Elain Thompson (Lerner Publications, 1998)
National Geographic Book of Mammals (National Geographic, 1998)
Big Cats (DK Eye Wonder) by Sarah Walker (Dorling Kindersley, 2002)

Cheetahs by Dianne M MacMillan (Carolrhoda Books, 1998)
Cheetahs by Melissa S Cole (Blackbirch Press, 2002)
Cheetahs: Spotted Speedsters by Jody Sullivan (Bridgestone Books, 2003)
Take-off! Really Wild: Cheetahs by Claire Robinson (Heinemann Library, 2002)

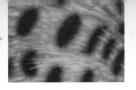

Index

Page numbers in **bold** refer to photographs or illustrations.